Wendy Cope Family Values

Walter de la Mare Selected Poems
Edited by Matthew Sweeney

Selected Poems
Edited by Peter Porter

James Fenton Yellow Tulips Poems 1968–2011

David Harsent Night

Michael Hofmann Selected Poems

Mick Imlah The Lost Leader

Emma Jones The Striped World

Paul Muldoon Maggot

Daljit Nagra Tippoo Sultan's Incredible White-Man-Eating Tiger Toy-Machine!!!

Alice Oswald Memorial

Don Paterson Rain

Chapcott Of Mutability

Stephen Spender New Collected Poems

Derek Walcott White Egrets

Hugo Williams West End Final

This diary belongs to

. . . .

First published in 2017
by Faber & Faber Ltd
Bloomsbury House
74–77 Great Russell Street
London WC1B 3DA

Designed and typeset by Faber & Faber Ltd
Printed in China by Imago

Clauses in the Banking and Financial Dealings Act allow the government
to alter dates at short notice

A CIP record for this book is available from the British Library

ISBN 978–0–571–33345–5

Faber
& Faber

Poetry
Planner

2018

JANUARY

M	T	W	T	F	S	S
1	2	3	4	5	6	7
8	9	10	11	12	13	14
15	16	17	18	19	20	21
22	23	24	25	26	27	28
29	30	31	1	2	3	4
5	6	7	8	9	10	11

FEBRUARY

M	T	W	T	F	S	S
29	30	31	1	2	3	4
5	6	7	8	9	10	11
12	13	14	15	16	17	18
19	20	21	22	23	24	25
26	27	28	1	2	3	4
5	6	7	8	9	10	11

MARCH

M	T	W	T	F	S	S
26	27	28	1	2	3	4
5	6	7	8	9	10	11
12	13	14	15	16	17	18
19	20	21	22	23	24	25
26	27	28	29	30	31	1
2	3	4	5	6	7	8

APRIL

M	T	W	T	F	S	S
26	27	28	29	30	31	1
2	3	4	5	6	7	8
9	10	11	12	13	14	15
16	17	18	19	20	21	22
23	24	25	26	27	28	29
30	1	2	3	4	5	6

MAY

M	T	W	T	F	S	S
30	1	2	3	4	5	6
7	8	9	10	11	12	13
14	15	16	17	18	19	20
21	22	23	24	25	26	27
28	29	30	31	1	2	3
4	5	6	7	8	9	10

JUNE

M	T	W	T	F	S	S
28	29	30	31	1	2	3
4	5	6	7	8	9	10
11	12	13	14	15	16	17
18	19	20	21	22	23	24
25	26	27	28	29	30	1
2	3	4	5	6	7	8

JULY

M	T	W	T	F	S	S
25	26	27	28	29	30	1
2	3	4	5	6	7	8
9	10	11	12	13	14	15
16	17	18	19	20	21	22
23	24	25	26	27	28	29
30	31	1	2	3	4	5

AUGUST

M	T	W	T	F	S	S
30	31	1	2	3	4	5
6	7	8	9	10	11	12
13	14	15	16	17	18	19
20	21	22	23	24	25	26
27	28	29	30	31	1	2
3	4	5	6	7	8	9

SEPTEMBER

M	T	W	T	F	S	S
27	28	29	30	31	1	2
3	4	5	6	7	8	9
10	11	12	13	14	15	16
17	18	19	20	21	22	23
24	25	26	27	28	29	30
1	2	3	4	5	6	7

OCTOBER

M	T	W	T	F	S	S
1	2	3	4	5	6	7
8	9	10	11	12	13	14
15	16	17	18	19	20	21
22	23	24	25	26	27	28
29	30	31	1	2	3	4
5	6	7	8	9	10	11

NOVEMBER

M	T	W	T	F	S	S
29	30	31	1	2	3	4
5	6	7	8	9	10	11
12	13	14	15	16	17	18
19	20	21	22	23	24	25
26	27	28	29	30	1	2
3	4	5	6	7	8	9

DECEMBER

M	T	W	T	F	S	S
26	27	28	29	30	1	2
3	4	5	6	7	8	9
10	11	12	13	14	15	16
17	18	19	20	21	22	23
24	25	26	27	28	29	30
31	1	2	3	4	5	6

JANUARY

M	T	W	T	F	S	S
26	27	28	29	30	31	1
2	3	4	5	6	7	8
9	10	11	12	13	14	15
16	17	18	19	20	21	22
23	24	25	26	27	28	29
30	31	1	2	3	4	5

FEBRUARY

M	T	W	T	F	S	S
30	31	1	2	3	4	5
6	7	8	9	10	11	12
13	14	15	16	17	18	19
20	21	22	23	24	25	26
27	28	1	2	3	4	5
6	7	8	9	10	11	12

MARCH

M	T	W	T	F	S	S
27	28	1	2	3	4	5
6	7	8	9	10	11	12
13	14	15	16	17	18	19
20	21	22	23	24	25	26
27	28	29	30	31	1	2
3	4	5	6	7	8	9

APRIL

M	T	W	T	F	S	S
27	28	29	30	31	1	2
3	4	5	6	7	8	9
10	11	12	13	14	15	16
17	18	19	20	21	22	23
24	25	26	27	28	29	30
1	2	3	4	5	6	7

MAY

M	T	W	T	F	S	S
1	2	3	4	5	6	7
8	9	10	11	12	13	14
15	16	17	18	19	20	21
22	23	24	25	26	27	28
29	30	31	1	2	3	4
5	6	7	8	9	10	11

JUNE

M	T	W	T	F	S	S
29	30	31	1	2	3	4
5	6	7	8	9	10	11
12	13	14	15	16	17	18
19	20	21	22	23	24	25
26	27	28	29	30	1	2
3	4	5	6	7	8	9

JULY

M	T	W	T	F	S	S
26	27	28	29	30	1	2
3	4	5	6	7	8	9
10	11	12	13	14	15	16
17	18	19	20	21	22	23
24	25	26	27	28	29	30
31	1	2	3	4	5	6

AUGUST

M	T	W	T	F	S	S
31	1	2	3	4	5	6
7	8	9	10	11	12	13
14	15	16	17	18	19	20
21	22	23	24	25	26	27
28	29	30	31	1	2	3
4	5	6	7	8	9	10

SEPTEMBER

M	T	W	T	F	S	S
28	29	30	31	1	2	3
4	5	6	7	8	9	10
11	12	13	14	15	16	17
18	19	20	21	22	23	24
25	26	27	28	29	30	1
2	3	4	5	6	7	8

OCTOBER

M	T	W	T	F	S	S
25	26	27	28	29	30	1
2	3	4	5	6	7	8
9	10	11	12	13	14	15
16	17	18	19	20	21	22
23	24	25	26	27	28	29
30	31	1	2	3	4	5

NOVEMBER

M	T	W	T	F	S	S
30	31	1	2	3	4	5
6	7	8	9	10	11	12
13	14	15	16	17	18	19
20	21	22	23	24	25	26
27	28	29	30	1	2	3
4	5	6	7	8	9	10

DECEMBER

M	T	W	T	F	S	S
27	28	29	30	1	2	3
4	5	6	7	8	9	10
11	12	13	14	15	16	17
18	19	20	21	22	23	24
25	26	27	28	29	30	31
1	2	3	4	5	6	7

JANUARY

M	T	W	T	F	S	S
31	1	2	3	4	5	6
7	8	9	10	11	12	13
14	15	16	17	18	19	20
21	22	23	24	25	26	27
28	29	30	31	1	2	3
4	5	6	7	8	9	10

FEBRUARY

M	T	W	T	F	S	S
28	29	30	31	1	2	3
4	5	6	7	8	9	10
11	12	13	14	15	16	17
18	19	20	21	22	23	24
25	26	27	28	1	2	3
4	5	6	7	8	9	10

MARCH

M	T	W	T	F	S	S
25	26	27	28	1	2	3
4	5	6	7	8	9	10
11	12	13	14	15	16	17
18	19	20	21	22	23	24
25	26	27	28	29	30	31
1	2	3	4	5	6	7

APRIL

M	T	W	T	F	S	S
25	26	27	28	29	30	31
1	2	3	4	5	6	7
8	9	10	11	12	13	14
15	16	17	18	19	20	21
22	23	24	25	26	27	28
29	30	1	2	3	4	5

MAY

M	T	W	T	F	S	S
29	30	1	2	3	4	5
6	7	8	9	10	11	12
13	14	15	16	17	18	19
20	21	22	23	24	25	26
27	28	29	30	31	1	2
3	4	5	6	7	8	9

JUNE

M	T	W	T	F	S	S
27	28	29	30	31	1	2
3	4	5	6	7	8	9
10	11	12	13	14	15	16
17	18	19	20	21	22	23
24	25	26	27	28	29	30
1	2	3	4	5	6	7

JULY

M	T	W	T	F	S	S
24	25	26	27	28	29	30
1	2	3	4	5	6	7
8	9	10	11	12	13	14
15	16	17	18	19	20	21
22	23	24	25	26	27	28
29	30	31	1	2	3	4

AUGUST

M	T	W	T	F	S	S
29	30	31	1	2	3	4
5	6	7	8	9	10	11
12	13	14	15	16	17	18
19	20	21	22	23	24	25
26	27	28	29	30	31	1
2	3	4	5	6	7	8

SEPTEMBER

M	T	W	T	F	S	S
26	27	28	29	30	31	1
2	3	4	5	6	7	8
9	10	11	12	13	14	15
16	17	18	19	20	21	22
23	24	25	26	27	28	29
30	1	2	3	4	5	6

OCTOBER

M	T	W	T	F	S	S
30	1	2	3	4	5	6
7	8	9	10	11	12	13
14	15	16	17	18	19	20
21	22	23	24	25	26	27
28	29	30	31	1	2	3
4	5	6	7	8	9	10

NOVEMBER

M	T	W	T	F	S	S
28	29	30	31	1	2	3
4	5	6	7	8	9	10
11	12	13	14	15	16	17
18	19	20	21	22	23	24
25	26	27	28	29	30	1
2	3	4	5	6	7	8

DECEMBER

M	T	W	T	F	S	S
25	26	27	28	29	30	1
2	3	4	5	6	7	8
9	10	11	12	13	14	15
16	17	18	19	20	21	22
23	24	25	26	27	28	29
30	31	1	2	3	4	5

PEARL
SIMON
ARMITAGE

1 Monday NEW YEAR'S DAY HOLIDAY (UK, IRL, AUS, ZA, NZ, CAN USA)

2 Tuesday 2ND JANUARY HOLIDAY (SCT)
DAY AFTER NEW YEAR'S DAY (NZ)

3 Wednesday

4 Thursday

Poly storm!

5 Friday ~~Fly to SMA~~ Did not, due to
storm on Thursday

6 Saturday

3 Kings Day!
Robin arrived

7 Sunday

Flew to Leon via
Houston
for SMA

A Soft-edged Reed of Light

That was the house where you asked me to remain
on the eve of my planned departure. Do you remember?
The house remembers it – the deal table
with the late September sun stretched on its back.
As long as you like, you said, and the chairs, the clock,
the diamond leaded lights in the pine-clad alcove
of that 1960s breakfast-room were our witnesses.
I had only meant to stay for a week
but you reached out a hand, the soft white cuff of your shirt
open at the wrist, and out in the yard,
the walls of the house considered themselves
in the murk of the lily-pond, and it was done.

Done. Whatever gods had bent to us then to whisper,
Here is your remedy – take it – here, your future,
either they lied or we misheard.
How changed we are now, how superior
after the end of it – the unborn children,
the mornings that came with a soft-edged reed of light
over and over, the empty rooms we woke to.
And yet if that same dark-haired boy
were to lean towards me now, with one shy hand
bathed in September sun, as if to say,
All things are possible – then why not this?
I'd take it still, praying it might be so.

8 Monday

First full day at SMA.
Saw my words on the wall at
Don Lupe.
3 King's Day Celebration

9 Tuesday

10 Wednesday

11 Thursday

12 Friday

13 Saturday   14 Sunday

Meeting Midnight

I met Midnight.
Her eyes were sparkling pavements after frost.
She wore a full-length, dark-blue raincoat with a hood.
She winked. She smoked a small cheroot.

I followed her.
Her walk was more a shuffle, more a dance.
She took the path to the river, down she went.
On Midnight's scent,
I heard the twelve cool syllables, her name,
chime from the town.
When those bells stopped,

Midnight paused by the water's edge.
She waited there.
I saw a girl in purple on the bridge.
It was One o'Clock.
Hurry, Midnight said. *It's late, it's late.*
I saw them run together.
Midnight wept.
They kissed full on the lips
and then I slept.

The next day I bumped into Half-Past Four.
He was a bore.

Carol Ann Duffy: New and Collected Poems for Children (2009)

15 Monday MARTIN LUTHER KING DAY (USA)

First night singing at ~~the~~ Don Lupe
- I Aint Skeered
- Other Countries
- Don Lupe

16 Tuesday

First night at the shelter. Cold and not well attended so I got to do 4 songs and they were: — I Aint Skeered   — Don Lupe
- Other Countries
- Someone Trying to Get Through

17 Wednesday

18 Thursday

19 Friday

20 Saturday   **21 Sunday**

Eyes that last I saw in tears

Eyes that last I saw in tears
Through division
Here in death's dream kingdom
The golden vision reappears
I see the eyes but not the tears
This is my affliction

This is my affliction
Eyes I shall not see again
Eyes of decision
Eyes I shall not see unless
At the door of death's other kingdom
Where, as in this,
The eyes outlast a little while
A little while outlast the tears
And hold us in derision.

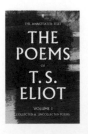

22 Monday

23 Tuesday

24 Wednesday

25 Thursday   BURNS NIGHT

26 Friday   AUSTRALIA DAY (AUS)

27 Saturday   28 Sunday

EDWIN MUIR

Collected

POEMS

29 Monday

30 Tuesday

31 Wednesday

1 Thursday

2 Friday

3 Saturday

4 Sunday

from Last Poems

XXXIII

When the eye of day is shut,
   And the stars deny their beams,
And about the forest hut
   Blows the roaring wood of dreams,

From deep clay, from desert rock,
   From the sunk sands of the main,
Come not at my door to knock,
   Hearts that loved me not again.

Sleep, be still, turn to your rest
   In the lands where you are laid;
In far lodgings east and west
   Lie down on the beds you made.

In gross marl, in blowing dust,
   In the drowned ooze of the sea,
Where you would not, lie you must,
   Lie you must, and not with me.

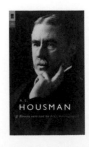

POET TO POET *A. E. Housman: Poems Selected by Alan Hollinghurst* (2005)

5 Monday Don Life

— Don Life
— Heavenly Aeroplan
— I Go To Pieces
— Grevous Angel

6 Tuesday WAITANGI DAY (NZ)

7 Wednesday

8 Thursday

9 Friday

10 Saturday   11 Sunday

The Boat

i.m. Seamus Heaney

Take the case of a man in a boat
in deep water. The wind and the waves
and the craft's tossing cause him to stumble
if he makes to stand up, for, no matter how firmly
he tries to hold on, through the boat's slithering
he bends and he staggers, so unstable
the body is. And yet he is safe.

It's the same with the righteous:
if they fall, they are falling only
like a man in a boat who is safe and sound
as long as he stays within the boat's timbers.

Piers Plowman, passus 8

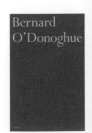

The Seasons of Cullen Church (2016)

1 2 Monday   LINCOLN'S BIRTHDAY

1 3 Tuesday

1 4 Wednesday   VALENTINE'S DAY

1 5 Thursday

1 6 Friday

1 7 Saturday   1 8 Sunday

infinity sincerity

For a guy who claims to hate cheesy stuff,
he proved true what he said before;
that for the girl he truly love,
he'll do anything possible to show.

All this while I've been loyal to LJ. Seriously,
LJ is very easy to manage. Just the html to edit,
hath thou forsaken me, that I am blind
and cannot see the simple truth

that dwells in me. They taught me how
to dodge and lie to hide my codes.
Cut and paste the here and there.
Forget what the intentions were . . .

Four brief years ago (it seems relevant)
I was a youth in college, but some of us
were looking at the Hummingbird Animal Totem.
I panicked and now I'm doing astrophysics.

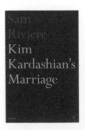

Kim Kardashian's Marriage (2015)

19 Monday PRESIDENTS' DAY (USA)

20 Tuesday

21 Wednesday

22 Thursday

23 Friday

24 Saturday   25 Sunday

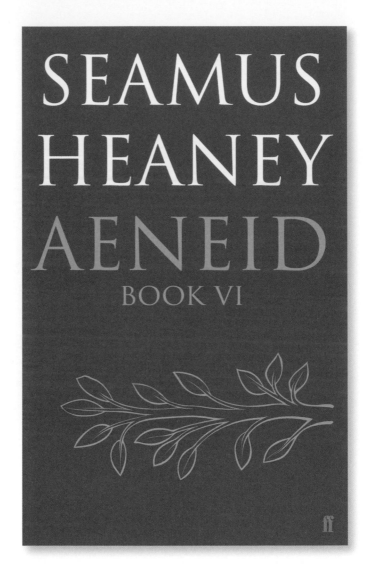

26 Monday

27 Tuesday

28 Wednesday

1 Thursday ST DAVID'S DAY

2 Friday

3 Saturday

4 Sunday

Young Lambs

The spring is coming by a many signs;
   The trays are up, the hedges broken down,
That fenced the haystack, and the remnant shines
   Like some old antique fragment weathered brown.
And where suns peep, in every sheltered place,
   The little early buttercups unfold
A glittering star or two – till many trace
   The edges of the blackthorn clumps in gold.
And then a little lamb bolts up behind
   The hill and wags his tail to meet the yoe,
And then another, sheltered from the wind,
   Lies all his length as dead – and lets me go
Close bye and never stirs but baking lies,
   With legs stretched out as though he could not rise.

5 Monday

6 Tuesday

7 Wednesday

8 Thursday

9 Friday

10 Saturday   11 Sunday

Sign of the Anchor

I stood at the dangerous shore.
Sleeves rolled up to my shoulders.
My fringe lifted in the wind in a long salute and I pushed it back.
Live your wish, Live your wish, said the sea.
I wanted to be like the shells on the beach, rubbed smooth and
 cracked open.
And I held my arms out, tipped my head back, pictured my
 protective symbols.
I opened my eyes and saw the sign of the anchor burning.
I had to go.
I shouted some words but they were lost when the waves crashed.
And ash rained from the sky.
I was far out, in wet denim, and the shore was a jolt when I
 looked back.

Stranger, Baby (2017)

12 Monday

13 Tuesday

14 Wednesday

15 Thursday

16 Friday

17 Saturday   ST PATRICK'S DAY   18 Sunday

Lines Written in Early Spring

I heard a thousand blended notes,
While in a grove I sate reclined,
In that sweet mood when pleasant thoughts
Bring sad thoughts to the mind.

To her fair works did Nature link
The human soul that through me ran;
And much it grieved my heart to think
What man has made of man.

Through primrose tufts, in that green bower,
The periwinkle trailed its wreaths;
And 'tis my faith that every flower
Enjoys the air it breathes.

The birds around me hopped and played,
Their thoughts I cannot measure: —
But the least motion which they made,
It seemed a thrill of pleasure.

The budding twigs spread out their fan,
To catch the breezy air;
And I must think, do all I can,
That there was pleasure there.

If this belief from heaven be sent,
If such be Nature's holy plan,
Have I not reason to lament
What man has made of man?

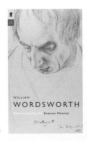

19 Monday ST PATRICK'S DAY HOLIDAY (IRL, NI)

20 Tuesday

21 Wednesday HUMAN RIGHTS DAY (ZA)

22 Thursday

23 Friday

24 Saturday   25 Sunday

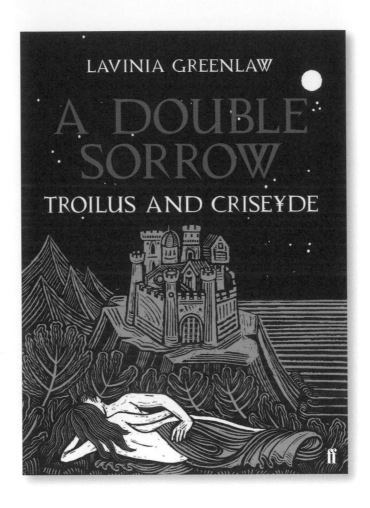

26 Monday

27 Tuesday

28 Wednesday

29 Thursday

30 Friday   GOOD FRIDAY (UK, AUS, ZA, NZ, CAN)

31 Saturday   EASTER (HOLY)   1 Sunday   EASTER SUNDAY (NZ)
                SATURDAY

One Day

To-day I have been happy. All the day
　I held the memory of you, and wove
Its laughter with the dancing light o' the spray,
　And sowed the sky with tiny clouds of love,
And sent you following the white waves of sea,
　And crowned your head with fancies, nothing worth,
Stray buds from that old dust of misery,
　Being glad with a new foolish quiet mirth.

So lightly I played with those dark memories,
　Just as a child, beneath the summer skies,
Plays hour by hour with a strange shining stone,
　For which (he knows not) towns were fire of old,
And love has been betrayed, and murder done,
　And great kings turned to a little bitter mould.

The Pacific, October 1913

2 Monday   EASTER MONDAY (UK NOT SCT, IRL, AUS, NZ)
FAMILY DAY (ZA)

3 Tuesday

4 Wednesday

5 Thursday

6 Friday

7 Saturday   8 Sunday

Sappho to Her Pupils

Live for the gifts the fragrant-breasted Muses
send, for the clear, the singing, lyre, my children.

Old age freezes my body, once so lithe,
rinses the darkness from my hair, now white.

My heart's heavy, my knees no longer keep me
up through the dance they used to prance like fawns in.

Oh, I grumble about it, but for what?
Nothing can stop a person's growing old.

Tithonus, as they tell, was swept away
in Dawn's passionate, rose-flushed arms to live

forever, but he lost his looks, his youth,
failing husband of an immortal bride.

with acknowledgements to the translation by Martin West

Lachlan
Mackinnon
Small
Hours

9   Monday

10   Tuesday

11   Wednesday

12   Thursday

13   Friday

14   Saturday   15   Sunday

Sonnet 19

Devouring Time, blunt thou the lion's paws,
And make the earth devour her own sweet brood;
Pluck the keen teeth from the fierce tiger's jaws,
And burn the long-lived phoenix in her blood;
Make glad and sorry seasons as thou fleet'st,
And do whate'er thou wilt, swift-footed Time,
To the wide world and all her fading sweets:
But I forbid thee one most heinous crime,
O carve not with thy hours my love's fair brow,
Nor draw no lines there with thine antique pen;
Him in thy course untainted do allow
For beauty's pattern to succeeding men.
    Yet do thy worst old Time: despite thy wrong,
    My love shall in my verse ever live young.

READING
SHAKESPEARE'S
SONNETS
A New Commentary by
Don Paterson

Reading Shakespeare's Sonnets: A New Commentary (2010)

16 Monday

17 Tuesday TAX DAY (USA)

18 Wednesday

19 Thursday

20 Friday

21 Saturday   22 Sunday

THE HAWK IN THE RAIN

poems

by

Ted Hughes

23 Monday ST GEORGE'S DAY

24 Tuesday

25 Wednesday ANZAC DAY (AUS, NZ)

26 Thursday

27 Friday FREEDOM DAY (ZA)

28 Saturday   29 Sunday

The Path

Running along a bank, a parapet
That saves from the precipitous wood below
The level road, there is a path. It serves
Children for looking down the long smooth steep,
Between the legs of beech and yew, to where
A fallen tree checks the sight: while men and women
Content themselves with the road and what they see
Over the bank, and what the children tell.
The path, winding like silver, trickles on,
Bordered and even invaded by thinnest moss
That tries to cover roots and crumbling chalk
With gold, olive, and emerald, but in vain.
The children wear it. They have flattened the bank
On top, and silvered it between the moss
With the current of their feet, year after year.
But the road is houseless, and leads not to school.
To see a child is rare there, and the eye
Has but the road, the wood that overhangs
And underyawns it, and the path that looks
As if it led on to some legendary
Or fancied place where men have wished to go
And stay; till, sudden, it ends where the wood ends.

Edward Thomas: Selected Poems (2011)

30 Monday

1 Tuesday   WORKERS' DAY (ZA)

2 Wednesday

3 Thursday

4 Friday

5 Saturday   6 Sunday

You're

Clownlike, happiest on your hands,
Feet to the stars, and moon-skulled,
Gilled like a fish. A common-sense
Thumbs-down on the dodo's mode.
Wrapped up in yourself like a spool,
Trawling your dark as owls do.
Mute as a turnip from the Fourth
Of July to All Fools' Day,
O high-riser, my little loaf.

Vague as fog and looked for like mail.
Farther off than Australia.
Bent-backed Atlas, our traveled prawn.
Snug as a bud and at home
Like a sprat in a pickle jug.
A creel of eels, all ripples.
Jumpy as a Mexican bean.
Right, like a well-done sum.
A clean slate, with your own face on.

Sylvia Plath: Poems Chosen by Carol Ann Duffy (2012)

7 Monday   EARLY MAY BANK HOLIDAY (UK)
            MAY DAY (IRL)

8 Tuesday

9 Wednesday

10 Thursday

11 Friday

12 Saturday   13 Sunday

On himselfe

I feare no Earthly Powers;
But care for crowns of flowers:
And love to have my Beard
With Wine and Oile besmear'd.
This day Ile drowne all sorrow;
Who knowes to live to morrow?

14 Monday

15 Tuesday

16 Wednesday

17 Thursday

18 Friday

19 Saturday   20 Sunday

THE TREE OF IDLE-NESS

LAWRENCE DURRELL

21 Monday

22 Tuesday

23 Wednesday

24 Thursday

25 Friday

26 Saturday   27 Sunday

You Are Definitely Coming, So Why Not Now?

after Akhmatova

Life is a frozen lamb: I'm waiting.
I have turned off the lights and been dramatic, opening doors.
Take any form you like.
Why not come thumping great chunks off us,
or cut our necks like bike locks,
or creep into our bodies like a smell in the fridge
or surprise our throats like a tune from the morning radio
that we'll notice we're singing the way you notice
a police car pulling up the drive?
I don't care how. The drains are gurgling,
the sky is a reservoir of wrong-headed questions. And eyes
that I love are losing their tournament.

Jack
Underwood
Happiness

28 Monday SPRING BANK HOLIDAY (UK), MEMORIAL DAY (USA)

29 Tuesday

30 Wednesday

31 Thursday

1 Friday

2 Saturday   3 Sunday

Roundelay

on all that strand
at end of day
steps sole sound
long sole sound
until unbidden stay
then no sound
on all that strand
long no sound
until unbidden go
steps sole sound
long sole sound
on all that strand
at end of day

Samuel Beckett: Collected Poems (2012)

4 Monday   JUNE BANK HOLIDAY (IRL), QUEEN'S BIRTHDAY HOLIDAY (NZ)

5 Tuesday

6 Wednesday

7 Thursday

8 Friday

9 Saturday   10 Sunday

'Sumer is icumen in'

Sumer is icumen in,
Loud sing cuckoo!
Groweth seed and bloweth mead
And springeth the wood now.
Sing cuckoo!

Ewe bleateth after lamb,
Cow loweth after calf,
Bullock starteth, buck farteth,
Merry sing cuckoo!

Cuckoo, cuckoo!
Well singest thou cuckoo,
Nor cease thou never now!

Sing cuckoo now, sing cuckoo!
Sing cuckoo, sing cuckoo now!

11 Monday

12 Tuesday

13 Wednesday

14 Thursday

15 Friday

16 Saturday   YOUTH DAY (ZA)   17 Sunday

THE ANNOTATED TEXT

THE
POEMS
OF
T. S.
ELIOT

VOLUME I

COLLECTED & UNCOLLECTED POEMS

18 Monday

19 Tuesday

20 Wednesday

21 Thursday

22 Friday

23 Saturday   24 Sunday

A Call

'Hold on,' she said, 'I'll just run out and get him.
The weather here's so good, he took the chance
To do a bit of weeding.'
                                    So I saw him
Down on his hands and knees beside the leek rig,
Touching, inspecting, separating one
Stalk from the other, gently pulling up
Everything not tapered, frail and leafless,
Pleased to feel each little weed-root break,
But rueful also . . .
                                    Then found myself listening to
The amplified grave ticking of hall clocks
Where the phone lay unattended in a calm
Of mirror glass and sunstruck pendulums . . .

And found myself then thinking: if it were nowadays,
This is how Death would summon Everyman.

Next thing he spoke and I nearly said I loved him.

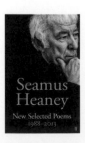

Seamus Heaney: New Selected Poems 1988–2013 (2014)

25 Monday

26 Tuesday

27 Wednesday

28 Thursday

29 Friday

30 Saturday   1 Sunday   CANADA DAY

The Oratory

I wouldn't swap my tree-haunt
in Tuam Inver for a mansion.
I've the stars to give me light,
the sun or moon as companion.

My cell's the work of craftsmen
known for providing shelter —
the dearest Lord of Heaven
is its architect and thatcher.

I've no fear of a downpour,
and no dread of battle spears
here under the ivy bower
where I've found a home outdoors.

*c.*800

The Finest Music: An Anthology of Early Irish Lyrics (2014)

2 **Monday** CANADA DAY HOLIDAY (CAN)

3 Tuesday

4 **Wednesday** INDEPENDENCE DAY (USA)

5 Thursday

6 Friday

7 Saturday 8 Sunday

Loch Music

I listen as recorded Bach
Restates the rhythms of a loch.
Through blends of dusk and dragonflies
A music settles on my eyes
Until I hear the living moors,
Sunk stones and shadowed conifers,
And what I hear is what I see,
A summer night's divinity.
And I am not administered
Tonight, but feel my life transferred
Beyond the realm of where I am
Into a personal extreme,
As on my wrist, my eager pulse
Counts out the blood of someone else.
Mist-moving trees proclaim a sense
Of sight without intelligence;
The intellects of water teach
A truth that's physical and rich.
I nourish nothing with the stars,
With minerals, as I disperse,
A scattering of quavered wash
As light against the wind as ash.

Douglas Dunn: New Selected Poems 1964–1999 (2003)

9 Monday

10 Tuesday

11 Wednesday

12 Thursday   BATTLE OF THE BOYNE HOLIDAY (NI)

13 Friday

14 Saturday   15 Sunday

FIGHTING TERMS

THOM GUNN

16 Monday

---

17 Tuesday

---

18 Wednesday

---

19 Thursday

---

20 Friday

---

21 Saturday   22 Sunday

Nature and Man

from Queen Mab

Look on yonder earth:
The golden harvests spring; the unfailing sun
Sheds light and life; the fruits, the flowers, the trees,
Arise in due succession; all things speak
Peace, harmony, and love. The universe,
In nature's silent eloquence, declares
That all fulfil the works of love and joy, –
All but the outcast man.

23 Monday

24 Tuesday

25 Wednesday

26 Thursday

27 Friday

28 Saturday   29 Sunday

Sunday Morning

Down the road someone is practising scales,
The notes like little fishes vanish with a wink of tails,
Man's heart expands to tinker with his car
For this is Sunday morning, Fate's great bazaar;
Regard these means as ends, concentrate on this Now,
And you may grow to music or drive beyond Hindhead anyhow,
Take corners on two wheels until you go so fast
That you can clutch a fringe or two of the windy past,
That you can abstract this day and make it to the week of time
A small eternity, a sonnet self-contained in rhyme.

But listen, up the road, something gulps, the church spire
Opens its eight bells out, skulls' mouths which will not tire
To tell how there is no music or movement which secures
Escape from the weekday time. Which deadens and endures.

Louis
MacNeice
Collected
Poems

Louis MacNeice: Collected Poems (2007)

30 Monday

31 Tuesday

1 Wednesday

2 Thursday

3 Friday

4 Saturday

5 Sunday

GREEK
METRE

AN INTRODUCTION

D.S.
RAVEN

FABER

6 Monday   AUGUST BANK HOLIDAY (IRL)

7 Tuesday

8 Wednesday

9 Thursday   NATIONAL WOMEN'S DAY HOLIDAY (ZA)

10 Friday

11 Saturday   12 Sunday

Full Moon and Little Frieda

A cool small evening shrunk to a dog bark and the clank of a bucket –

And you listening.
A spider's web, tense for the dew's touch.
A pail lifted, still and brimming – mirror
To tempt a first star to a tremor.

Cows are going home in the lane there, looping the hedges with
    their warm wreaths of breath –
A dark river of blood, many boulders,
Balancing unspilled milk.

'Moon!' you cry suddenly, 'Moon! Moon!'

The moon has stepped back like an artist gazing amazed at a work

That points at him amazed.

Ted Hughes: Collected Poems (2003)

13 Monday

14 Tuesday

15 Wednesday

16 Thursday

17 Friday

18 Saturday

19 Sunday

The Song of Wandering Aengus

I went out to the hazel wood,
Because a fire was in my head,
And cut and peeled a hazel wand,
And hooked a berry to a thread;
And when white moths were on the wing,
And moth-like stars were flickering out,
I dropped the berry in a stream
And caught a little silver trout.

When I had laid it on the floor
I went to blow the fire aflame,
But something rustled on the floor,
And some one called me by my name:
It had become a glimmering girl
With apple blossom in her hair
Who called me by my name and ran
And faded through the brightening air.

Though I am old with wandering
Through hollow lands and hilly lands,
I will find out where she has gone,
And kiss her lips and take her hands;
And walk among long dappled grass,
And pluck till time and times are done
The silver apples of the moon,
The golden apples of the sun.

20 Monday

21 Tuesday

22 Wednesday

23 Thursday

24 Friday

25 Saturday   26 Sunday

Garments

from a prose poem by C. P. Cavafy

In an old trunk or in an ebony chest
I put away the yellow clothes of my childhood,
my favourite yellow clothes.

I put away the blue clothes I wore as a boy,
the blue clothes that boys always wear,
followed by the red clothes of my youth,

the exciting red clothes of a young man.
I put away the red clothes, then I put away
the blue clothes again, more faded this time.

I wear black clothes. I live in a black house.
Sometimes at night I open the ebony chest
and gaze with longing at my beautiful clothes.

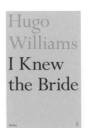

I Knew the Bride (2014)

27 Monday   SUMMER BANK HOLIDAY (UK)

28 Tuesday

29 Wednesday

30 Thursday

31 Friday

1 Saturday   2 Sunday

Hurrahing in Harvest

Summer ends now; now, barbarous in beauty, the stooks rise
Around; up above, what wind-walks! what lovely behaviour
Of silk-sack clouds! has wilder, wilful-wavier
Meal-drift moulded ever and melted across skies?

I walk, I lift up, I lift up heart, eyes,
Down all that glory in the heavens to glean our Saviour;
And, éyes, heárt, what looks, what lips yet gave you a
Rapturous love's greeting of realer, of rounder replies?

And the azurous hung hills are his world-wielding shoulder
Majestic – as a stallion stalwart, very-violet-sweet! –
These things, these things were here and but the beholder
Wanting; which two when they once meet,
The heart rears wings bold and bolder
And hurls for him, O half hurls earth for him off under
   his feet.

3 Monday   LABOR DAY (USA), LABOUR DAY (CAN)

4 Tuesday

5 Wednesday

6 Thursday

7 Friday

8 Saturday   9 Sunday

CAROL ANN
DUFFY

· IRELAND · A · LAUREATE'S · CHOICE · OF · THE · POETRY · OF · BRITAIN · AND ·

The Map
and the
Clock

GILLIAN
CLARKE

ff

10 Monday   ROSH HASHANAH

11 Tuesday

12 Wednesday

13 Thursday

14 Friday

15 Saturday   16 Sunday

The Sick Rose

O Rose thou art sick.
The invisible worm,
That flies in the night
In the howling storm:

Has found out thy bed
Of crimson joy:
And his dark secret love
Does thy life destroy.

POET TO POET *William Blake: Poems Selected by James Fenton* (2010)

17 Monday

18 Tuesday

19 Wednesday   YOM KIPPUR

20 Thursday

21 Friday

22 Saturday   23 Sunday

from To Autumn

Season of mists and mellow fruitfulness,
　　Close bosom-friend of the maturing sun,
Conspiring with him how to load and bless
　　With fruit the vines that round the thatch-eves run;
To bend with apples the mossed cottage-trees,
　　And fill all fruit with ripeness to the core;
　　　To swell the gourd, and plump the hazel shells
　　With a sweet kernel; to set budding more,
And still more, later flowers for the bees,
Until they think warm days will never cease,
　　　For Summer has o'er-brimmed their clammy cells.

Who hath not seen thee oft amid thy store?
　　Sometimes whoever seeks abroad may find
Thee sitting careless on a granary floor,
　　Thy hair soft-lifted by the winnowing wind;
Or on a half-reaped furrow sound asleep,
　　Drowsed with the fume of poppies, while thy hook
　　　Spares the next swath and all its twinèd flowers;
And sometimes like a gleaner thou dost keep
　　Steady thy laden head across a brook;
　　Or by a cider-press, with patient look,
　　　Thou watchest the last oozings hours by hours.

24 Monday   HERITAGE DAY (ZA)

25 Tuesday

26 Wednesday

27 Thursday

28 Friday

29 Saturday   30 Sunday

Spellbound

The night is darkening round me,
The wild winds coldly blow;
But a tyrant spell has bound me
And I cannot, cannot go.

The giant trees are bending
Their bare boughs weighed with snow.
And the storm is fast descending,
And yet I cannot go.

Clouds beyond clouds above me,
Wastes beyond wastes below;
But nothing drear can move me;
I will not, cannot go.

Short and Sweet: 101 Very Short Poems (1999)

1 Monday

2 Tuesday

3 Wednesday

4 Thursday

5 Friday

6 Saturday

7 Sunday

Daljit Nagra
Tippoo Sultan's Incredible White-Man-Eating Tiger Toy-Machine!!!

Poetry

ff

8 Monday THANKSGIVING DAY (CAN), COLUMBUS DAY (USA)

9 Tuesday

10 Wednesday

11 Thursday

12 Friday

13 Saturday 14 Sunday

In My Dreams

In my dreams I am always saying goodbye and riding away,
Whither and why I know not nor do I care.
And the parting is sweet and the parting over is sweeter,
And sweetest of all is the night and the rushing air.

In my dreams they are always waving their hands and saying
    goodbye,
And they give me the stirrup cup and I smile as I drink,
I am glad the journey is set, I am glad I am going,
I am glad, I am glad, that my friends don't know what I think.

The Collected Poems and Drawings of Stevie Smith (2015)

15 Monday

16 Tuesday

17 Wednesday

18 Thursday

19 Friday

20 Saturday   21 Sunday

Daybreak

At dawn she lay with her profile at that angle
Which, sleeping, seems the stone face of an angel;
Her hair a harp the hand of a breeze follows
To play, against the white cloud of the pillows.
Then in a flush of rose she woke, and her eyes were open
Swimming with blue through the rose flesh of dawn.
From her dew of lips, the drop of one word
Fell, from a dawn of fountains, when she murmured
'Darling', – upon my heart the song of the first bird.
'My dream glides in my dream,' she said, 'come true.
I waken from you to my dream of you.'
O, then my waking dream dared to assume
The audacity of her sleep. Our dreams
Flowed into each other's arms, like streams.

Stephen
Spender
New
Collected
Poems

22 Monday LABOUR DAY (NZ)

23 Tuesday

24 Wednesday

25 Thursday

26 Friday

27 Saturday   28 Sunday

Song. To Celia

Drinke to me, onely, with thine eyes,
    And I will pledge with mine;
Or leave a kisse but in the cup,
    And Ile not looke for wine.
The thirst, that from the soule doth rise,
    Doth aske a drinke divine:
But might I of JOVE'S *Nectar* sup,
    I would not change for thine.
I sent thee, late, a rosie wreath,
    Not so much honouring thee,
As giving it a hope, that there
    It could not withered bee.
But thou thereon didst onely breath,
    And sent'st it backe to mee;
Since when it growes, and smells, I sweare,
    Not of it selfe, but thee.

29 Monday   OCTOBER BANK HOLIDAY (IRL)

30 Tuesday

31 Wednesday   HALLOWEEN

1 Thursday

2 Friday

3 Saturday   4 Sunday

5 Monday

---

6 Tuesday

---

7 Wednesday

---

8 Thursday

---

9 Friday

---

10 Saturday

11 Sunday   REMEMBRANCE SUNDAY
VETERANS DAY (USA)

November

No sun – no moon!
No morn – no noon –
No dawn –
No sky – no earthly view –
No distance looking blue –
No road – no street – no 't'other side the way' –
No end to any Row –
No indications where the Crescents go –
No top to any steeple –
No recognitions of familiar people –
No courtesies for showing 'em –
No knowing 'em!
No traveling at all – no locomotion,
No inkling of the way – no notion –
'No go' – by land or ocean –
No mail – no post –
No news from any foreign coast –
No park – no ring – no afternoon gentility –
No company – no nobility –
No warmth, no cheerfulness, no healthful ease,
No comfortable feel in any member –
No shade, no shine, no butterflies, no bees,
No fruits, no flowers, no leaves, no birds,
November!

12 Monday   VETERANS DAY HOLIDAY (USA)

---

13 Tuesday

---

14 Wednesday

---

15 Thursday

---

16 Friday

---

17 Saturday   18 Sunday

Brueghel's Two Monkeys

This is what I see in my dreams about final exams:
two monkeys, chained to the floor, sit on the windowsill,
the sky behind them flutters,
the sea is taking its bath.

The exam is History of Mankind.
I stammer and hedge.

One monkey stares and listens with mocking disdain,
the other seems to be dreaming away—
but when it's clear I don't know what to say
he prompts me with a gentle
clinking of his chain.

View with a Grain of Sand (1996)

19 Monday

20 Tuesday

21 Wednesday

22 Thursday   THANKSGIVING DAY (USA)

23 Friday

24 Saturday   25 Sunday

Birds in Winter

I know not what small winter birds these are,
Warbling their hearts out in that dusky glade
While the pale lustre of the morning star
　　In heaven begins to fade.

Not me they sing for, this — earth's shortest — day,
A human listening at his window-glass;
They would, affrighted, cease and flit away
　　At glimpse even of my face.

And yet how strangely mine their music seems,
As if of all things loved my heart was heir,
Had helped create them — albeit in my dreams —
　　And they disdained my share.

Walter de la Mare: Selected Poems (2006)

26 Monday

27 Tuesday

28 Wednesday

29 Thursday

30 Friday ST ANDREW'S DAY HOLIDAY (SCT)

1 Saturday   2 Sunday

3 Monday   HANUKKAH (FIRST DAY)

4 Tuesday

5 Wednesday

6 Thursday

7 Friday

8 Saturday   9 Sunday

The Mower

The mower stalled, twice; kneeling, I found
A hedgehog jammed up against the blades,
Killed. It had been in the long grass.

I had seen it before, and even fed it, once.
Now I had mauled its unobtrusive world
Unmendably. Burial was no help:

Next morning I got up and it did not.
The first day after a death, the new absence
Is always the same; we should be careful

Of each other, we should be kind
While there is still time.

Philip Larkin: The Complete Poems (2012)

10 Monday

11 Tuesday

12 Wednesday

13 Thursday

14 Friday

15 Saturday

16 Sunday DAY OF
RECONCILIATION (ZA)

Mid-Winter

Cut flowers in a vase this night,
orange, golden and snow-white;
dark green leaves and darker stems,
take me where the dark earth bends
its darkened forehead to the east,
where Lucy lights the candles for her feast.

Gethsemane Day (2006)

Dorothy
Molloy
Gethsemane
Day

17 Monday   DAY OF RECONCILIATION HOLIDAY (ZA)

18 Tuesday

19 Wednesday

20 Thursday

21 Friday

22 Saturday   23 Sunday

'I stood on a tower in the wet'

I stood on a tower in the wet,
And New Year and Old Year met,
And winds were roaring and blowing;
And I said, 'O years, that meet in tears,
Have ye aught that is worth the knowing?
Science enough and exploring,
Wanderers coming and going,
Matter enough for deploring,
But aught that is worth the knowing?'
Seas at my feet were flowing,
Waves on the shingle pouring,
Old Year roaring and blowing,
And New Year blowing and roaring.

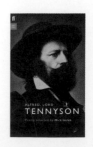

POET TO POET *Alfred, Lord Tennyson: Poems Selected by Mick Imlah* (2004)

24 Monday   CHRISTMAS EVE

25 Tuesday   CHRISTMAS DAY (UK, IRL, AUS, NZ, ZA, CAN, USA)

26 Wednesday   BOXING DAY (UK, AUS, NZ), ST STEPHEN'S DAY (IRL),
DAY OF GOODWILL (ZA)

27 Thursday

28 Friday

29 Saturday   30 Sunday

31 Monday   NEW YEAR'S EVE

1 Tuesday   NEW YEAR'S DAY (UK, IRL, AUS, ZA, NZ, CAN, USA)

2 Wednesday   2ND JANUARY HOLIDAY (SCT), DAY AFTER NEW YEAR'S DAY (NZ)

3 Thursday

4 Friday

5 Saturday   6 Sunday

A Brief Chronology of Faber's Poetry Publishing

1925 Geoffrey Faber acquires an interest in The Scientific Press and renames the firm Faber and Gwyer. ¶ The poet/bank clerk T. S. Eliot is recruited. 'What will impress my directors favourably is the sense that in you we have found a man who combines literary gifts with business instincts.' – Geoffrey Faber to T. S. Eliot ¶ Eliot brought with him *The Criterion*, the quarterly periodical he had been editing since 1922. (*The Waste Land* had appeared in its first issue, brilliantly establishing its reputation.) He continued to edit it from the Faber offices until it closed in 1939. Though unprofitable, it was hugely influential, introducing early work by Auden, Empson and Spender, among others, and promoting many notable European writers, including Proust and Valéry. ¶ Publication of T. S. Eliot's *Poems, 1909–1925*, which included *The Waste Land* and a new sequence, *The Hollow Men*. ¶

1927 From 1927 to 1931 Faber publishes a series of illustrated pamphlets known as *The Ariel Poems* containing unpublished poems by an eminent poet (Thomas Hardy, W. B. Yeats, Harold Monro, Edith Sitwell and Edmund Blunden, to name but a few) along with an illustration, usually in colour, by a leading contemporary artist (including Eric Gill, Eric Ravilious, Paul Nash and Graham Sutherland). ¶

1928 Faber and Gwyer announce the *Selected Poems of Ezra Pound*, with an introduction and notes by Eliot. ¶

1929 Geoffrey Faber buys out Lady Gwyer and oversees the birth of the Faber and Faber imprint. Legend has it that Walter de la Mare, the father of Faber director Richard de la Mare, suggested the euphonious repetition: another Faber in the company name 'because you can't have too much of a good thing'. ¶

1930 W. H. Auden becomes a Faber poet with a collection entitled simply *Poems*. ¶ Eliot publishes *Ash Wednesday*. ¶

1933 Stephen Spender becomes a Faber poet with his first collection *Poems*, a companion piece to Auden's 1930 work of the same name. ¶ The first British edition of James Joyce's *Pomes Penyeach* is published. ¶

1935 The American poet Marianne Moore publishes with Faber. 'Miss Moore's poems form part of a small body of durable poetry written in our time.' – T. S. Eliot ¶ Louis MacNeice becomes a Faber poet. 'The most original Irish poet of his generation.' – Faber catalogue 1935 ¶

1936 The hugely influential *Faber Book of Modern Verse* (edited by Michael Roberts) is published. ¶

1937 *In Parenthesis* by David Jones is published. 'This is an epic of war. But it is like no other war-book because for the first time that experience has been reduced to "a shape in words." The impression still remains that this book is one of the most remarkable literary achievements of our time.' – *Times Literary Supplement* ¶ W. H. Auden is awarded the Queen's Gold Medal for Poetry. ¶

1939 T. S. Eliot's *Old Possum's Book of Practical Cats* is published with a book jacket illustrated by the author. Originally called *Pollicle Dogs and Jellicle Cats*, the poems were written for his five godchildren. The eldest of these was Geoffrey Faber's son Tom – himself much later a director of Faber and Faber. ¶

1944 Walter de la Mare's *Peacock Pie* is published with illustrations by Edward Ardizzone. ¶ Philip Larkin's first novel, *A Girl in Winter*, is published. 'A young man with an exceptionally clear sense of what, as a writer, he means to do.' – *Times Literary Supplement* ¶

1948 T. S. Eliot wins the Nobel Prize in Literature. ¶

1949 Ezra Pound's *Pisan Cantos* is published. 'The most incomprehensible passages are often more stimulating than much comprehensibility which passes for poetry today.' – *Times Literary Supplement* ¶

1954 *The Ariel Poems* are revived with a new set of pamphlets by W. H. Auden, Stephen Spender, Louis MacNeice, T. S. Eliot, Walter de la Mare, Cecil Day Lewis and Roy Campbell. The artists include Edward Ardizzone, Edward Bawden, Michael Ayrton and John Piper. ¶

1957 Ted Hughes comes to Faber with *The Hawk in the Rain*. ¶ Siegfried Sassoon receives the Queen's Gold Medal for Poetry. ¶

1959 Robert Lowell's collection *Life Studies* is published. ¶

1960 Saint-John Perse wins the Nobel Prize in Literature. ¶

1961 Geoffrey Faber dies. ¶ Ted Hughes's first collection of children's poems, *Meet My Folks*, is published. ¶

1963 Sylvia Plath's novel *The Bell Jar* is published by Faber in the year of her death. ¶ The Geoffrey Faber Memorial Prize is established as an annual prize awarded in alternating years to a single volume of poetry or fiction by a Commonwealth author under forty. ¶

1964 Philip Larkin's *The Whitsun Weddings* is published. ¶

1965 T. S. Eliot dies. ¶ Sylvia Plath's posthumous collection, *Ariel*, is published. 'Her extraordinary achievement, poised as she was between volatile emotional state and the edge of the precipice.' – Frieda Hughes ¶ Philip Larkin is awarded the Queen's Gold Medal for Poetry. ¶

1966 Seamus Heaney comes to Faber with *Death of a Naturalist*. ¶

1968 Ted Hughes's *The Iron Man* is published. ¶

1971 Stephen Spender is awarded the Queen's Gold Medal for Poetry. ¶

1973 Paul Muldoon comes to Faber with his first collection, *New Weather*. ¶

1974 Ted Hughes receives the Queen's Gold Medal for Poetry. ¶

1977 Tom Paulin comes to Faber with his first collection, *A State of Justice*. ¶ Norman Nicholson receives the Queen's Gold Medal for Poetry. ¶

1980 Czesław Miłosz wins the Nobel Prize in Literature. ¶

1981 *Cats*, the Andrew Lloyd Webber musical based on *Old Possum's Book of Practical Cats*, opens in London. ¶

1984 *Rich*, a collection by Faber's own poetry editor, Craig Raine, is published. 'Puts us in touch with life as unexpectedly and joyfully as early Pasternak.' – John Bayley ¶ Ted Hughes becomes Poet Laureate. ¶

1985 Douglas Dunn's collection *Elegies* is the Whitbread Book of the Year. ¶

1986 Vikram Seth's *The Golden Gate* is published. ¶

1987 Seamus Heaney's *The Haw Lantern* wins the Whitbread Poetry Award. ¶

1988 Derek Walcott is awarded the Queen's Gold Medal for Poetry. ¶

1992 Derek Walcott wins the Nobel Prize in Literature. ¶ Thom Gunn's collection *The Man with the Night Sweats* wins the Forward Poetry Prize for Best Collection, while Simon Armitage's *Kid* wins Best First Collection. ¶

1993 Andrew Motion wins the Whitbread Biography Award for his book on Philip Larkin. ¶ Don Paterson's *Nil Nil* wins the Forward Poetry Prize for Best First Collection. ¶

1994 Paul Muldoon wins the T. S. Eliot Prize for *The Annals of Chile*. ¶ Alice Oswald wins an Eric Gregory Award. ¶

1995 Seamus Heaney wins the Nobel Prize in Literature. ¶

1996 Wisława Szymborska wins the Nobel Prize in Literature. ¶ Seamus Heaney's *The Spirit Level* wins the Whitbread Poetry Award. 'Touched by a sense of wonder.' – Blake Morrison ¶

1997 Don Paterson wins the T. S. Eliot Prize for *God's Gift to Women*. ¶ Lavinia Greenlaw wins the Forward Prize for Best Single Poem for 'A World Where News Travelled Slowly'. ¶ Ted Hughes's *Tales from Ovid* is the Whitbread Book of the Year. 'A breathtaking book.' – John Carey ¶

1998 Ted Hughes wins the Whitbread Book of the Year for the second time running with *Birthday Letters*, which also wins the T. S. Eliot Prize. 'Language like lava, its molten turmoils hardening into jagged shapes.' – John Carey ¶ Ted Hughes is awarded the Order of Merit. ¶ Christopher Logue receives the Wilfred Owen Poetry Award. ¶

1999 Seamus Heaney's *Beowulf* wins the Whitbread Book of the Year Award. '[Heaney is the] one living poet who can rightly claim to be Beowulf's heir.' – *New York Times* ¶ A memorial service for Ted Hughes is held at Westminster Abbey. In his speech Seamus Heaney calls Hughes 'a guardian spirit of the land and language'. ¶ Hugo Williams wins the T. S. Eliot Prize for his collection *Billy's Rain*. ¶ Andrew Motion is appointed Poet Laureate. ¶

2000 Seamus Heaney receives the Wilfred Owen Poetry Award. ¶

2002 Alice Oswald wins the T. S. Eliot Prize for Poetry for her collection *Dart*. ¶

2003 Paul Muldoon is awarded the Pulitzer Prize for Poetry for *Moy Sand and Gravel*. *Landing Light* by Don Paterson wins the Whitbread Poetry Award. ¶

2004 August Kleinzahler receives the International Griffin Poetry Prize for *The Strange Hours Travellers Keep*. ¶ Hugo Williams is awarded the Queen's Gold Medal for Poetry. ¶

2005 David Harsent wins the Forward Prize for Best Collection for *Legion*. ¶ Harold Pinter receives the Wilfred Owen Poetry Award. ¶ Charles Simic receives the International Griffin Poetry Prize for *Selected Poems 1963–2003*. ¶ Nick Laird wins an Eric Gregory Award. ¶

2006 Christopher Logue wins the Whitbread Poetry Award for *Cold Calls*. ¶ The Geoffrey Faber Memorial Prize is awarded to Alice Oswald for *Woods Etc*. ¶ Seamus Heaney wins the T. S. Eliot Prize for *District and Circle*. ¶

2007 Tony Harrison is awarded the Wilfred Owen Poetry Award. ¶ Daljit Nagra wins the Forward Prize for Best First Collection for *Look We Have Coming to Dover!* ¶ James Fenton receives the Queen's Gold Medal for Poetry. ¶

2008 Daljit Nagra wins the South Bank Show / Arts Council Decibel Award. ¶ Mick Imlah's collection *The Lost Leader* wins the Forward Prize for Best Collection. ¶

2009 Carol Ann Duffy becomes Poet Laureate. ¶ Don Paterson's *Rain* wins the Forward Poetry Prize for Best Collection while *The Striped World* by Emma Jones wins the Best First Collection Prize. ¶

2010 *The Song of Lunch* by Christopher Reid is shortlisted for the Ted Hughes Award for New Work in Poetry and he is awarded the Costa Poetry Award for *A Scattering*. ¶ The John Florio Prize for Italian Translation 2010 is awarded to Jamie McKendrick for *The Embrace*. ¶ Derek Walcott wins both the Warwick Prize and the T. S. Eliot Prize for Poetry for his collection *White Egrets*. ¶ *Rain* by Don Paterson is shortlisted for the Saltire Scottish Book of the Year. ¶ Tony Harrison is awarded the Prix Européen de Littérature. ¶ The Keats–Shelley Prize is awarded to Simon Armitage for his poem 'The Present'. ¶ The Forward Prize for Best Collection is awarded to Seamus Heaney for *Human Chain*. ¶ Also shortlisted for the Forward Prize for Best Collection are Lachlan Mackinnon for *Small Hours* and Jo Shapcott for *Of Mutability*. ¶ The Centre for Literacy in Primary Education (CLPE) Poetry Prize is awarded to Carol Ann Duffy for *New and Collected Poems for Children*. ¶ Alice Oswald wins the Ted Hughes Award for New Work in Poetry for *Weeds and Wild Flowers*. ¶ *The Striped World* by Emma Jones is shortlisted for the Adelaide Festival Poetry Award. ¶ The Queen's Gold Medal for Poetry is awarded to Don Paterson. ¶

2011 *Of Mutability* by Jo Shapcott is the Costa Book of the Year. ¶ *Human Chain* by Seamus Heaney and *Maggot* by Paul Muldoon are both shortlisted for the *Irish Times* Poetry Now Award. ¶ *Night* by David Harsent is shortlisted for the Forward Prize for Best Collection. ¶ 'Bees' by Jo Shapcott is shortlisted for the Forward Prize for Best Single Poem. ¶ A new digital edition of T. S. Eliot's *The Waste Land* for iPad is launched, bringing to life one of the most revolutionary poems of the last hundred years, illuminated by a wealth of interactive features. ¶ The Queen's Gold Medal for Poetry is awarded to Jo Shapcott. ¶ At Westminster Abbey a memorial is dedicated to Ted Hughes in Poets' Corner. ¶

2012 *The Death of King Arthur* by Simon Armitage is shortlisted for the T. S. Eliot Prize. ¶ *The World's Two Smallest Humans* by Julia Copus is shortlisted for the T. S. Eliot Prize and the Costa Poetry Award. ¶ David Harsent's collection *Night* wins the International Griffin Poetry Prize. ¶ *81 Austerities* by Sam Riviere wins the Felix Dennis Prize for Best First Collection, one of the Forward Prizes for Poetry. ¶ *Farmers Cross* by Bernard O'Donoghue is shortlisted for the *Irish Times* Poetry Now Award. ¶

2013 The Forward Prize for Best First Collection is awarded to Emily Berry for *Dear Boy*. ¶ Hugo Williams is shortlisted for the Forward Prize for Best Single

Poem for 'From the Dialysis Ward'. ¶ Alice Oswald is awarded the Warwick Prize for Writing for her collection *Memorial*, which also wins the Poetry Society's Corneliu M. Popescu Prize for poetry in translation. ¶ The Queen's Gold Medal for Poetry is awarded to Douglas Dunn. ¶ The shortlist for the T. S. Eliot Prize includes Daljit Nagra for *The Ramayana: A Retelling* and Maurice Riordan for *The Water Stealer.* ¶ *Pink Mist* by Owen Sheers wins the Hay Festival Medal for Poetry. ¶ In his eulogy for Seamus Heaney, Paul Muldoon says, 'We remember the beauty of Seamus Heaney – as a bard, and in his being.' In November the first official tribute evenings to Heaney are held at Harvard, then in New York, followed by events at the Royal Festival Hall in London, the Waterfront Hall, Belfast, and the Sheldonian, Oxford. ¶

2014 Maurice Riordan is shortlisted for the Pigott Poetry Prize for *The Water Stealer.* ¶ Hugo Williams is shortlisted for the Forward Prize for Best Collection for *I Knew the Bride.* ¶ Daljit Nagra is awarded the Society of Authors Travelling Scholarship. ¶ Nick Laird's *Go Giants* is shortlisted for the *Irish Times* Poetry Now Award. ¶ Emily Berry, Emma Jones and Daljit Nagra are announced as three of the Poetry Book Society's Next Generation Poets 2014. ¶ *Pink Mist* by Owen Sheers is named the Wales Book of the Year after winning the poetry category. ¶

2015 *Fire Songs* by David Harsent is awarded the T. S. Eliot Prize for Poetry. ¶ Alice Oswald wins the Ted Hughes Award for New Work for *Tithonus*, a poem and performance commissioned by London's Southbank Centre. ¶ *One Thousand Things Worth Knowing* by Paul Muldoon wins the Pigott Poetry Prize. ¶ Don Paterson is awarded the Neustadt International Prize for Literature. ¶ *Terror* by Toby Martinez de las Rivas is shortlisted for the Seamus Heaney Centre for Poetry's Prize for First Full Collection. ¶ Paul Muldoon's *One Thousand Things Worth Knowing* is shortlisted for the Forward Prize for Best Collection. ¶ James Fenton is awarded the Pen Pinter Prize. ¶ *40 Sonnets* by Don Paterson wins the Costa Poetry Award, and is short-listed for the T. S. Eliot Prize. ¶

2016 Don Paterson is shortlisted for the International Griffin Poetry Prize. ¶ *40 Sonnets* by Don Paterson is short-listed for the Saltire Society Literary Awards. ¶ *The Seasons of Cullen Church* by Bernard O'Donohue is shortlisted for the T. S. Eliot Prize. ¶ Jack Underwood receives a Somerset Maugham Award. ¶ An excerpt from *Salt* by David Harsent is shortlisted for the Forward Prize for Best Single Poem. ¶

Acknowledgements

Poetry

All poetry reprinted by permission of Faber & Faber alone unless otherwise stated.

'A Soft-edged Reed of Light' taken from *The World's Two Smallest Humans* © Julia Copus.

'Meeting Midnight' taken from *New and Collected Poems for Children* © Carol Ann Duffy 2014. Reproduced by permission of the author c/o Rogers, Coleridge & White Ltd., 20 Powis Mews, London, W11 1JN.

'Eyes that last I saw in tears' taken from *Collected Poems 1909–1962* © Set Copyrights Limited. Reprinted by permission of Faber & Faber Ltd. Copyright 1936 by Houghton Mifflin Harcourt Publishing Company. Copyright © renewed 1964 by Thomas Stearns Eliot. Reprinted by permission of Houghton Mifflin Harcourt Publishing Company. All rights reserved.

'The Boat' taken from *The Seasons of Cullen Church* © Bernard O'Donoghue.

'infinity sincerity' taken from *Kim Kardashian's Marriage* © Sam Riviere.

'Sign of the Anchor' taken from *Stranger, Baby* © Emily Berry.

'Sappho to Her Pupils' taken from *Small Hours* © Lachlan Mackinnon.

'You're' taken from *Collected Poems* © The Estate of Sylvia Plath. Reprinted by permission of Faber & Faber Ltd., and HarperCollins Publishers, New York.

'You are Definitely Coming, So Why Not Now?' taken from *Happiness* © Jack Underwood.

'Roundelay' from *The Collected Poems of Samuel Beckett*, copyright (c) 1930, 1935, 1961, 1977, 1989 by Samuel Beckett. Copyright © 2012 by the Estate of Samuel Beckett. Copyright © 1978, 1992 by Samuel Beckett/Editions de Minuit. Used by permission of Grove/Atlantic, Inc. and Faber & Faber Ltd. Any third party use of this material, outside of this publication, is prohibited.

'A Call' taken from *New Selected Poems 1988–2013* © The Estate of Seamus Heaney. Reprinted by permission of Faber & Faber Ltd., and Farrar Straus & Giroux, LLC., New York.

'The Oratory' taken from *The Finest Music: An Anthology of Early Irish Lyrics* © Maurice Riordan.

'Loch Music' taken from *New Selected Poems 1964–1999* © Douglas Dunn.

'Sunday Morning' taken from *Collected Poems* © The Estate of Louis MacNeice. Reprinted by permission of David Higham Associates, London.

'Full Moon and Little Frieda' taken from *Collected Poems* © The Estate of Ted Hughes. Reprinted by permission of Faber & Faber Ltd., and Farrar, Straus & Giroux, LLC., New York.

'Garments' taken from *I Knew the Bride* © Hugo Williams.

'In My Dreams' taken from *Collected Poems of Stevie Smith* copyright © 1972 by Stevie Smith. Reprinted by permission of Faber & Faber Ltd., and New Directions Publishing Corp.

'Daybreak' taken from *New Collected Poems* © 2004. Reprinted by kind permission of the Estate of Stephen Spender.

'Brueghel's Two Monkeys' from *View with a Grain of Sand: Selected Poems*, translated from the Polish by Stanisław Barańczak and Clare Cavanagh © The Estate of Wisława Szymborska. Reprinted by permission of Faber & Faber Ltd. Copyright © 1995 by Houghton Mifflin Harcourt

Picture Credits

NOTES

NOTES

NOTES

FABER MEMBERS

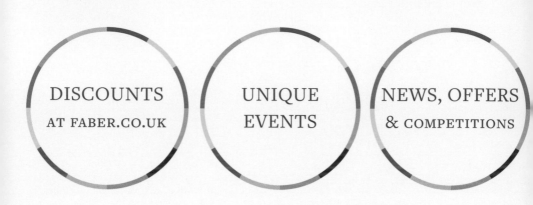

DISCOUNTS AT FABER.CO.UK

UNIQUE EVENTS

NEWS, OFFERS & COMPETITIONS

Faber Members is an award-winning, free-to-join programme for people who love books.

Sign up today for discounts on books at **faber.co.uk**, access to unique events and news, special offers and exclusive competitions.

TO DO
- ~~Pick up S from Karate~~
- ~~Call Dad about plants~~

- CONJURE NEW WORLDS

Start *your* story today . . .

When you've got an idea for a story, it can be hard to find the time to get it down on paper. Our creative writing courses can help you make the most of every little window. Whatever else is going on. Call us today – 0207 927 3827.

FABER ACADEMY
– writing courses with *character* –

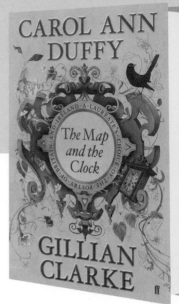

Simon Armitage
Book
of Matches

Simon
Armitage
Seeing
Stars

W. H. Auden
The Dyer's
Hand

W. H.
Auden
Selected
Poems
Revised Edition
Edited by Edward Mende

Mark Ford
Soft Sift

Matthew
Francis
Muscovy

Lavinia
Greenlaw
The
Casual
Perfect

Ian
Hamilto
Collecte
Poems
Edited by Alan Jenkins

James Joyce
Poems
and Shorter
Writings
Edited by Richard Ellmann
A. Walton Litz and
John Whittier-Ferguson

Nick
Laird
Go
Giants

Logue's Homer
Cold Calls
War Music continued

Andrew
Motion
The
Cinder
Path

Don
Paterson
Selected
Poems

Sylvia Plath
Ariel

Ezra
Pound
Selected
Poems
1908–1969

Christoph
Reid
Nonsense